Gullible's Travels

Leadership Lessons for Your Journey Through Life's Jungle

D0644482

TOPPER LONG

Gullible's Travels

Leadership Lessons for Your Journey
Through Life's Jungle

Copyright © 2008 Topper Long. All rights reserved.

No part of this book may be reproduced in any form without written permission in advance from the publisher. International rights and foreign translations available only through negotiation with CornerStone Leadership Institute.

Inquiries regarding permission for use of the material contained in this book should be addressed to:

CornerStone Leadership Institute
P.O. Box 764087
Dallas, TX 75376
888.789.LEAD

Printed in the United States of America
ISBN: 978-0-9798009-6-2

Credits

Collaborative Editor	Alice Adams, Austin, TX
	rtadams2@aol.com
Copy Editor	Kathleen Green, Positively Proofed, Plano, TX
	info@PositivelyProofed.com
Design, art direction, and production	Melissa Monogue, Back Porch Creative, Plano, TX
	info@BackPorchCreative.com

TABLE OF CONTENTS

THE CHALLENGES OF THE SAFARI

It's a jungle out there, and life in the jungle changes fast!

Let me introduce myself.

People call me *Gullible*, which means "easily deceived or duped." This name came about because of my naïve belief that life should be the way I want it to be rather than the way it really is. This gullibility has been a life-long trait, leading me to take things at face value, believe most people are good and honest and, all the while, maintaining a generally positive attitude.

Every day, we're all traveling through many jungles, and all jungles have two things in common: mysteries and surprises.

We also encounter many diverse people and situations that make travel and survival in the jungles difficult. And every day, we are expected to travel through the jungles faster and faster. We cannot leisurely walk through the jungle. We need to run ... and run *FAST*!

My journey through life's jungle, although interesting and exciting, has brought many challenges ... challenges of deception, unfulfilled promises and unexpected results. However, it's also been a journey of growth and reward filled with opportunities to learn many valuable lessons along the way.

I wanted to share these lessons with you because it *is* a jungle out there, and these lessons and tips can help you survive and be successful on your personal safari.

———————————

There once was a world where life was much simpler and much slower. In that *business* jungle, you gave your heart, mind, body and often your soul to the company, and the company took care of you for life. You communicated in person or with letters and phone calls. There were no computers or cell phones with e-mails and text messages.

In that long-ago world, almost every product and technology anywhere in the world originated in the United States. Close enough was often good enough. More people agreed more often on what was right and what was wrong, and it seemed as though you had time to think about your actions.

THAT WORLD NO LONGER EXISTS!

The jungle has changed and survival in today's jungle demands that we constantly learn and change. In my travels, I've found people generally resist both learning and changing because it's often stressful and difficult.

However, if we are to enjoy our journey, we must embrace learning and changing while we define standards for our lives, then stick to them. That, too, is very stressful and difficult.

Knowing when to change and when to stick is more complicated than ever. My travels have spanned both the "old world" and the "new." I have learned the importance of learning and changing through my personal experience in the jungle.

Many years ago, I earned a Master's degree in Executive Management. But I found that most of my valuable lessons have come from trial and error, success and failure, good mentoring – the School of Experience. That is what this book is about.

With much support and help, I have successfully survived my most difficult and stressful journeys, and I have enjoyed most of the trip. I hope that the lessons I have learned and the tips I'll share will help you survive the jungle *and* allow you to enjoy your journey.

FLYING OVER THE JUNGLE

"Oh, would the gift the Giver give us,
to see ourselves as others see us."
ROBERT BURNS

Mrs. Doran was my high school language teacher. She was a small woman with a serious – almost stern – demeanor but a deep love for the minds and souls of all her students.

When I did something in her class that I thought was much cuter than she did, Mrs. Doran would look at me and simply say, *"Would the gift the Giver give us, to see ourselves as others see us."* I heard her say this many times!

I thought it was strange then, but for all the years since high school, these words have been invaluable. She was telling me she didn't see me as I saw myself. No matter how cute I thought I was, she did not agree ... and, unfortunately for me, she had the only vote that counted.

Perception is reality to its owner. Each of us deals with two perceptions critical to our success and our happiness: how others see us and how we see ourselves.

Regardless of our intentions, it is perception that matters in how others relate to us or how they see us. My perception of myself influences my behavior and my behavior influences others' perception of me.

Sound confusing? Let me explain from my life's safari as a business leader.

My father was a good leader and, inheriting many of his traits, I began leading others at an early age – blessed with common sense, the ability to think fast on my feet and a positive self-image. I also enjoy being in front of people and attacking the most difficult situations … and, quite honestly, enjoy leading more than following.

Whether as president of a class, an officer in the Army or CEO of a company, accepting the leadership role was always pretty easy. I saw myself as the ideal leader – listening, approachable, caring, open, truthful, responsive, supportive, forgiving, eloquent – all those good attributes … and more.

What contributed to my belief? Maybe it was because I saw myself that way and was receiving what appeared to be genuine, positive responses. The more those responses came, the more I was convinced the good characteristics existed and the more those beliefs influenced my behavior. Thus, it became a never-ending cycle.

I had "positive jobs" leading teams doing positive things for most of my career … jobs that were generally stable and good experiences. Sure, there were a few "wild animals in the jungle" – natural and easily recognizable enemies. Sometimes we sparred, which was at times oddly enjoyable, and as the old saying goes, "You win a few, you lose a few," but it was all in a day's work.

As time passed, the number of team members expanded from a few to many, and the jobs and challenges became bigger and harder.

From all appearances, my leadership was successful because there was never a serious mutiny. My team seemed comfortable following my lead, we got where we were going ... and the journey was usually fun as well as rewarding.

There was never mutiny at home, either. We moved all over the country and my family would pack up, get into the car, and wonder, "Where are we going now?" Even with this constant family uprooting, we had no serious arguments, our marriage survived all the changes and we had fun and learned a lot along the way.

Then, things changed!

For the remaining years of my career, I was a "hatchet man," the guy who did the jobs others didn't want to do – or could not do. My new role meant I had to reorganize, downsize, right-size, close plants, fire people, lay people off and move people from their lifelong homes – totally disrupting, and sometimes destroying, life as they had known it. But, all these things were done in such a humane way!

Warning the hatchet's victims far in advance and eloquently explaining those slaughters in detail, I then provided support systems to help them recover from the carnage.

We had picnics and meetings to keep them all informed on how the injured were being rehabilitated and how nicely the situation was improving. We had staff meetings in which the animals were remarkably agreeable. Nobody said anything negative, and everybody was very polite and agreeable.

Yes. I'll admit there were times I found it necessary to have a bodyguard living in or near my home, but I actually thought all of the employees who survived liked me. How gullible was that?

Imagine my shock when I learned those above, around and below me in this corporate jungle had widely varying views of me as a person and as a leader. None completely agreed with my view of myself. Some came close to agreeing with my view of myself and some – okay, many – did not see me that way at all.

My intentions and aspirations to possess all of those desirable characteristics of an ideal leader did not make a difference in what the team believed about me or about my intentions. **Their perception was their reality – and they had good reasons to believe what they believed** ... about me, their company and their jobs.

After a series of leadership miscalculations, two of my remaining faithful followers told me what was going to happen – my own massacre was close at hand. My associates, including most of those closest to me, were actively participating in a coup to dismantle the organization I had worked five years to build.

I was shocked, then angry and, finally, devastated. How could they all be such rabid cannibals?

Because I could not accept the situation, I rather loudly extracted myself from it. It took long, honest and painful introspection to analyze and understand what had happened.

The bottom line: I had repeatedly failed to realize that their collective view of me did not match my view of myself. The signs were there, some of them big, flashing-red signs, but I had ignored them all.

From these events, I learned four valuable lessons about the importance of seeing yourself as others see you:

1. **Perceptions are realities to their owners.**

2. **People relate to you based on their perceptions and not on your intentions.**

3. **It is more important to know their perceptions than your intentions.**

4. **Make sure the perceptions and the realities are what you are proud to have the world see.**

As a leader, your goal is to be informed of the true situation and to match your team's perceptions with your intentions.

Okay, by now you may be asking yourself two questions: "How could this guy have been so gullible ... and *so wrong*?" and, "If he is that gullible and that wrong, why should I listen to him?"

Both are valid questions.

First, I did not always do the things I am going to suggest that you do. Second, if you continue to read about the things I did right and what I learned, you may be able to do them while also avoiding some of my mistakes.

So how do we find out how others see us? How do we avoid our own Armageddon – the unexpected massacre of our herd and ourselves?

Learn to "fly over the jungle." You cannot see an accurate picture of the jungle when you are in the middle of it. You have to get above the jungle and look down at the big picture through the eyes of someone else. You have to picture yourself in their part of the jungle. Be truthful. No cheating or fibbing.

Many times, I did not fly over my jungle nor did I look at the big picture. I did not honestly put myself in the jungles of others – jungles I had created – but you can.

The first thing you have to do is surround yourself with people who will tell you the truth, even if it hurts. In his book, *Orchestrating Attitude*, Lee Colan advises to "Build your BEST team – Buddies who Ensure Success and Truth." Surrounding yourself with the BEST people will keep you honest and your feet on the ground. Honestly learn how your team perceives you so that you can see yourself as others see you.

I often surrounded myself with people who were not my BEST team. They were good people but not the right people to help us achieve our goals. They told me what I wanted to hear rather than what I needed to hear. I didn't surround myself with my BEST team, but you can.

One of the toughest lessons to accept is that, as a leader, your intentions or reality may never completely match the perceptions of others. Maybe this happens because you know things others don't know or you have to consider things the rest of the team doesn't have to consider. You know these things because you are in a leadership position. It is your job to skillfully integrate them into your decisions and make those decisions without hesitation, apologies or lengthy explanations. It's your job of leadership.

However, when you're flying over the jungle, you can more clearly see that things are not the way they appear when you're on the ground, including warning signs that danger lies ahead. If you have made a habit of ignoring these signs, open your eyes ... now! Then, think about incorporating the following new habits into your journey:

+ **If you don't like what you see or hear, have the honesty, humility, courage and determination to change your behavior.**

+ **Behave so others will see you the way you want them to see you – and the way you want to see yourself.**

+ **Work hard to align the perceptions of others with your perception of yourself and your reality.**

+ **Be consistent. Match the perceptions of others with your honest intentions and reality, deliver what you promise and live seamlessly (as we'll discuss in the next chapter).**

My mistake was that I never took the time to fly over the jungle and never saw the "Danger Ahead" sign that would have warned me that the situation was not as I thought it was. By the time I was told what was happening, it was too late. The die had been cast and the plot developed. The massacre was imminent.

You can avoid the massacre of your team – or even your own slaughter – if you learn to fly over the jungle and see yourself as others see you.

LESSONS:

1. Perceptions are realities to their owners.

2. People relate to you based on their perceptions – and not on your intentions.

3. It is extremely important to know the perceptions of those you're leading.

4. Make sure the perceptions, intentions and realities that others notice are things you are proud of.

TIPS:

1. Fly over the jungle – and pay attention to what you see below.

2. Surround yourself with your "BEST" team and listen to them.

3. Honestly learn how people perceive you – to see yourself as others see you.

4. Have the honesty, humility, courage and determination to change your behavior and match others' perceptions with your intentions and to reality.

CHAPTER 2

SEAMLESS LIVING

*The real secret to genuine happiness
is living the same way every day.*

My dad was a wonderful man, but he had the bad habit of "cussin,"
as we called it in the South.

I well remember my seventh birthday party when all my little
friends from church and school were gathered around our dining
table for cake and ice cream. My dad had taken off from work
early to attend.

At one of my happiest moments, he said something profane – I don't
remember what – but, in an instant, the party was in shambles.
My mom, my friends, and I were mortified. Resuscitation was
impossible – the party was dead.

His poor judgment and behavior also impacted him and he began, at that very moment, to watch his tongue more closely, although he never completely succeeded.

As a result, and because my dad was always my hero, I, at an early age, accepted cursing as something real men did.

I don't remember when I started "cussin," but it was long before I was in the seventh grade because, by then, I was already good at it. That's when I told Ralph, the class bully, if he picked on Charles like he was picking on me, Charles would "beat the hell out of him."

I said that in Mr. Buffington's class and Ralph immediately told on me in front of the whole class. I got sent to the principal's office and got two spankings that day: one from the principal and another at home. That was before schools got sued and neighbors called Social Services when a kid got a spanking.

Needless to say, those spankings didn't stop me because cursing was cool and it made you look big.

Most of the boys and even some of the girls did it. Cursing remained cool in high school and in college, in the Army and at work, so I kept doing it for years.

I never cursed at home and, certainly, not at church or in front of anybody I really respected – just with the other cool, cursing folks around me whom I wanted to impress.

I also developed the skill of telling jokes and stories I would not have dreamed of telling at home. I was so good at it, I boasted of my ability to tell a joke based on any word of the listener's choice. Sometimes I had to change a word or two in the joke to make it work, but I could do it … and, in certain circles, I was the life of the party where others gathered around to test my skills and listen to my stories. It was great! I got a lot of attention!

There I was, the wise, old owl of colorful jokes, surrounded by a bunch of laughing hyenas, and I reveled at my ability to capture an audience … even an audience of hyenas.

I don't remember, exactly, when I tried to stop using profanity and telling colorful jokes and stories, but I remember the circumstances very well.

I had been a key participant in a business meeting and afterwards, Mike Hergert, a young man who reported to me, came to me and asked to speak to me privately. We found a space and Mike said, "You're a good guy with high standards, but you sure didn't talk like one in that meeting. You're better than that!"

What courage that took for Mike and what a profound impact it had on me!

At that point, I realized I had a choice to make. Until then, I had tried to lead two lives and I secretly felt guilt in both of them. When I was at home or at church, I felt guilty because of the way I behaved at work. When I was at work, I felt guilty because I knew my language, including the profanity and the kinds of jokes I was good at telling, didn't feel right.

I also realized, at that point, the people I really wanted to impress were not impressed by profanity and dirty jokes.

For the leader of quality people, profanity is a sign of weakness, not strength. Using it demonstrates a subconscious belief you cannot lead effectively without profanity's shock value. If you are a leader and you use profanity, do you really believe that you cannot lead without profanity? I doubt it!

One of the basic leadership lessons is that "Everything Counts." Every word you say, how you say it, and everything you do has an impact on somebody … even when you think no one is listening or really cares what you are saying or doing. **You never know who is listening or who you are influencing.**

So I started cleaning up my act but, for a curse-aholic, it wasn't easy to do. Old habits that predate seventh grade are hard to break … and, as the world around me gets more tolerant, more vulgar and less easily offended by anything, it somehow has become more acceptable to lead two lives. But it doesn't work if you want to be truly happy and content.

Al Lovelady, a wonderful friend and mentor, once told me contentment is "the quiet acceptance of God's plan for your life." Now, how can I be quietly accepting God's plan for my life if I am behaving different ways on different days?

It took me a long time to finally realize that the only way to be content with my life is to work hard at developing what I call a "seamless life," trying to live the same way every day everywhere – seamless. No breaks, no different hats, no different standards.

If you are living a seamless life, it is one life. You walk your talk wherever you are, whatever you are doing. The lessons and tips in this book are not just for your business life, your family life, your neighborhood life or any of your other lives. They are for your seamless life, where everybody – including you – sees the same you whenever they see you and wherever you are.

About 10 years ago, at the annual meeting of the management and staff of the organization I was leading, there was a question-and-answer session near the end of the day. Throughout the meeting, we had discussed business, career development and other topics, including personal ethics and values. We'd also developed and committed to a Leadership Agreement, which read:

LEADERSHIP AGREEMENT

As leaders, we commit to Doing What's Right.

DOING WHAT'S RIGHT is...

+ recognizing and accepting our responsibilities, individually and collectively;
+ being positive contributors in achieving our goals;
+ using our corporate values as our guide;
+ leading by example and following when required;
+ accepting change in the pursuit of excellence.

It had been a good day and everybody was relaxed and comfortable. Sitting on a stool at the front of the room, I invited anybody to ask me anything about anything.

That's when somebody asked, "What is the one most important thing I should remember if I want to be successful?"

What a loaded question! After some thought, I finally said, "Let me ask you a question. What do you want on your tombstone?"

This was long before the popular pizza commercial, so nobody laughed and the room fell silent. Most were wondering if I had lost my mind. What do tombstones have to do with business or success?

After more silence, I felt compelled to explain that a tombstone is unique. It summarizes your entire life in one sentence. We spent more than an hour talking about a lot of serious and personal issues. Then, everybody took a piece of paper and wrote what he/she wanted on their tombstone – how they wanted to be remembered … in 20 words or less.

I wrote, "A man of integrity who helped a few people along the way."

We did not share what we wrote that day and I have not shared what I wrote with many people between that day and now, but what I wrote has driven me to do at least one good and unexpected deed each day.

I encourage you to think about and then decide what you want on your tombstone – your final epitaph. Write it down, make copies and put them on your desk, your bathroom mirror, refrigerator door and on your dashboard. Become guided by what you have written.

Every person is different and every epitaph unique. Your epitaph should be your own. The important part is to have a crystal clear understanding of your life goal and live with your specific goal in mind, all day every day, wherever you are. When you write your epitaph, you can more easily begin living a seamless life toward it.

Many people struggle to find their life's goal. To help you discover your life goal, it may help to ask yourself some questions:

- ✦ "What will be on the tombstones of my best friends? My mentors? My worst enemies?"
- ✦ "What would other people write on my tombstone?"
- ✦ "Would what others write on my tombstone be different from what I want written?"

If the answer to that last question is "Yes," you probably still have work to do in defining and living your seamless life. Begin by flying over the jungle and keeping your life seamless with your BEST team's help. It's the only way you are going to be genuinely happy and able to fulfill your dreams.

LESSONS:

1. Be true to yourself.

2. You never know whom you are influencing ... or when or where.

3. The key to happiness and contentment is living a seamless life.

4. The seamless life is one life – business, family, church, social – all the same life.

TIPS:

1. Think and decide today what you want on your tombstone.

2. Write down what you want on your tombstone and post reminders everywhere.

3. Become guided by what you have written – all day, every day.

4. Fly over your jungle, using your BEST team to keep your life seamless. Live so that what you want on your tombstone will eventually be inscribed on it.

BALANCING THE FOUR P'S

*The key secret for success in living a happy, seamless life is achieving and maintaining a **BALANCE** between **Four P's** – **P**rogress, **P**erfection, **P**ulling Together and **P**ositive Attitude – in all aspects of your life.*

Anytime you trek through the business jungle, your survival depends on having an experienced guide to show you the way. I have had many great guides in my life, but I want to introduce you to three in particular. They have contributed immeasurably to what you are reading in this book.

I introduce them now because the concept of "Balancing the Four P's" is the cornerstone of my life … and these three mentors are responsible for the birth, development and growth of the concept of "Balancing the Four P's."

I hope you have good guides on your own travels through the jungles. If you don't, find some good ones because we all desperately need them. Even though my dad had that bad habit of "cussin," he was the mentor and guide who influenced my life and belief structure the most. He died at the age of 61, and while he was a simple and humble man, Dad was bigger than life to me. As a kid and long after childhood, I stayed as close to him as I could.

He was never "not cool" to me or my friends. He was our buddy and we obeyed him out of respect. We wanted to be around him and we wanted him to be proud of us.

My dad was a one-man BEST team. He knew how to do so many things. He taught me to do a lot of them, some very well. He taught me how to be a carpenter, a woodworker, a plumber, an electrician and a mechanic. I still use all of those skills today.

He had his first job, a paper route, at age six and all of his earnings went to support his family. He rode a motorcycle through an open manhole early one dark morning while delivering papers and was nearly killed. Ironically, the one thing he did not teach me nor allow me to do was ride a motorcycle.

He learned many of life's lessons the hard way – and earlier than most. He had only a high school education but he was street smart with amazing native intelligence, and he shared his knowledge and wisdom with others.

My dad was the first to teach me the concept of "Balancing the Four P's," although he would never have called it that. I didn't realize it had come from him until I began writing this book.

He believed in making **progress**, striving for **perfection, pulling together** and having a **positive attitude** … and he was **balanced** in that he believed in trying to do all four in equal proportions.

My second guide, who overlapped my dad by about 10 years – and continues the work he began after he left us – is my wife, Carole.

Carole and I have been married 45 years. We have been poor together and we have been rich together. We have raised two wonderful daughters. We have laughed together, cried together, been afraid together, been excited together, and have shared many lengthy journeys together.

Carole has relocated our household 17 times without complaint. She's accompanied me through many very good and not-so-good treks through the jungle ... and she's also been the source of some of my most valuable lessons about life.

In 1993, we were in a strange and unfamiliar place, and I was close to losing a job that I had desired my entire career. I felt vulnerable – more vulnerable than ever in my life and I was truly afraid. So Carole sat with me, held my hand and said simply, "We started out living in a mobile home with very little, so we know we can do it. If we have to do it again, we'll just have as much fun as we had the first time."

We prayed, took a nap, had a nice dinner, and I was not afraid any more. I didn't lose my job and went on to finish my career. But, if I had lost that job, we would have done as she said we would do ... and I was prepared to do it.

I am a person of extremes – hot or cold, good or bad, happy or mad, sick or well, I like you or I don't – nothing in between. Carole's not like that. She shares many of my dad's good characteristics, one of which is balance.

Carole is much more patient and forgiving than I and, certainly, less extreme. Her favorite mantra is, simply, "Balance."

Carole has spent her life trying to balance me ... and she's right. One of the most important lessons we can learn is to lead a balanced life.

———————————

The third guide on my journey through life's jungle was John Kleban. John was very different from my dad or Carole ... a good thing because he taught me things the others could not.

My dad and wife were patient, caring and definitely softer. John, on the other hand, was more ferocious. He was stronger, faster, smarter, more volatile and definitely was not cuddly!

He loved a good fight and would tear another human being to shreds in an instant, if threatened. He was also a successful big-game hunter and a consummate businessman.

Having an IQ of nearly 200, a photographic memory and a vast knowledge of all aspects of business, John was a genius. And, he was my boss for 10 years before his untimely death at the young age of 53.

I never knew he even liked me until two weeks before he died, but he taught me more about business than anyone else I met during my career. It was a privilege and constant lesson to follow him, and I learned from him many of the business lessons and tips I am sharing with you now.

At the end of a particularly bad week in the spring of 1990, John called me to his farm one Saturday morning. I had been among those attending a meeting the day before when he had attacked the group and then simply left the room in anger.

I knew, as I mowed my lawn later that day, it was not over. He was simply resting, plotting a new strategy of business death for the unlucky.

Our Saturday meeting took place in John's game room, surrounded by the heads of several large animals he had killed on his many big-game safaris. It seemed an appropriate place for such a meeting.

We talked for several hours about the problems that had surfaced the day before. At the end of our meeting, John assigned me the task of taking three warring organizations and making them effective. He told me I could do whatever I wanted with them … as long as I fixed the problems and kept him informed of what I was doing.

This should have been a sign he liked and trusted me, but somehow it wasn't. In John's presence, even as he stood in cut-off jeans and a T-shirt, I felt strangely like just another hapless wildebeest being shoved to the head of the herd.

This meeting also marked the beginning of my career as the "hatchet man."

Two weeks later, the warring organizations had been consolidated into one and more than a third of the people had been fired. It was also at this point, and after nearly 30 years of "balance mentoring" – by my dad and Carole – that the concept of "Balancing the Four P's" came to life.

I first presented it to the 64 people in our new organization. I didn't know, at that time, how permanent it would become in my life and the lives of many others.

At that meeting, I used a crude, hand-drawn picture of a kitchen knife with four sweet peas balanced on the blade to illustrate the concept.

Shortly after that, I realized how crucial balancing the Four P's is to achieving a seamless life. After introducing "Balancing the Four P's," I soon fashioned a four-arm balance beam with one of the Four P's on each arm. That logo became my leadership trademark, which I later copyrighted and used as a rallying tool in nearly every discussion, formal or informal, for the remainder of my career.

To my delight, in a short period of time our team soon adopted it as the theme. Soon it was everywhere – notepads, T-shirts, and murals on cafeteria walls. There were also white business cards with just the logo and bright red cards developed by some of our team that read:

BALANCING THE FOUR P's

PULLING TOGETHER means teamwork, open communication, sharing ideas and working together to make us the best we can be collectively.

PERFECTION means doing it right every time, on time; our goal is perfection in everything we do.

POSITIVE ATTITUDE means finding the good in your particular situation; being a part of the solution rather than part of the problem. Positive attitudes are contagious.

PROGRESS means not focusing on where we've been, but working toward a successful future.

There are five keywords in "Balancing the Four P's": Balance, Progress, Perfection, Pulling, and Positive.

Seeking Progress and Perfection, Pulling Together and having a Positive Attitude are individually important, but the crucial aspect is in achieving a Balance among them.

Good Realtors know the three key secrets to success in real estate are location, location and location. Similarly, the three key secrets to successfully achieving a happy, seamless life are balance, balance and balance.

If I obsess on one or two of the Four P's at the expense of the others, the results can be disastrous ... so let's look briefly at what can happen:

Suppose an obsession for **Progress** tips the scale.

Think for a moment – how is progress typically measured? Progress seems to be all about money – more profit, return on investment and more cash this quarter than last quarter or the same quarter last year. Right?

If we focus only on progress, we don't worry about developing infrastructure for the long term, giving good service, having a better product for our customers or striving for Perfection. We don't worry about developing a team and taking care of the people who are making our money for us – Pulling Together. We don't worry about having a Positive Attitude about anything other than making progress. Just make Progress! Just make more money! The long-term result is disaster!

———————————

Suppose an obsession for **Perfection** tips the scale.

Here are some of the symptoms: Nothing ever gets finished because we never finish improving. We have study groups, consultants and lots of meetings to discuss how we can improve. Engineering and development costs soar with no income to support them. People argue endlessly over the minutiae necessary to get that "extra percent" of whatever. For those wanting to actually do something, attitudes go to the basement and frustration runs rampant throughout the herd. The long-term result is disaster!

———————————

Suppose an obsession for **Pulling Together** tips the scale.

Let's make sure we are all on the same team. Wow! An organization-wide love-in! This brings lots of off-site meetings, retreats, team-building exercises on ropes courses, picnics and more consultants – but for "teamwork development" training this time.

Bureaucracies and organizational charts emerge. Meanwhile, nothing is getting done that makes money, which is – remember – the measure of progress. The product or service is suffering because we are all working on pulling together instead of seeking perfection in what we do … and again, the positive attitudes tank for those who came to actually work. The long-term result is disaster!

Finally, suppose an obsession for **Positive Attitude** tips the scale.

Let's make sure we are all happy. Let's give everybody whatever it takes to make – and keep – them happy: longer breaks, more time off, more money, promotions, big bonuses, stock options, free health benefits … whatever it takes to keep them happy.

Everyone may be happy for a while but when costs soar and products and services suffer, we will eventually lose customers. People who see what's coming leave with smiles on their faces and we eventually go out of business. That's when all of those positive attitudes tend to quickly become negative. The long-term result is disaster!

Two important points: First, all of the above illustrations seem extreme but are taken from actual experiences during my career. I have personally experienced each and every one of them but not all at one time. It is impossible to be obsessed with all four P's at the same time! But I have experienced obsessions with each of them many times, as I am sure you have.

And, when these situations developed and were noted, that's when the hatchet man came onto the scene. That's why achieving and maintaining balance is the key.

Second, I have used illustrations from my business life, but I could just as easily have used similar illustrations from other areas of my life. When we allow things to get out of balance in our personal lives, the results are frequently divorce, suicide and abuse. When things get seriously out of balance and stay there, the long-term result is disaster.

LESSONS:

1. Making Progress, seeking Perfection, Pulling Together, and having a Positive Attitude are key ingredients for having a happy, seamless life and productive career.

2. Achieving and maintaining BALANCE among the Four P's is the secret to the success of the process.

TIPS:

1. Find, cultivate and use good guides as you travel through the jungle.

2. Spend time analyzing the weight that each of the Four P's has in all of your "lives."

3. Balance! Balance! Balance!

CHAPTER 4

PROGRESS: RIDING A RHINO

Rhinos keep charging ...
no matter how much resistance they face!

To help others and myself keep focused on making progress, I had two unframed posters tacked to my office wall. One was of a lone ship far out at sea with a quote from Charlie Shedd: *"A ship in the harbor is safe, but that's not what ships are built for."*

The second poster showed three hippopotamuses standing motionless in a marsh with their mouths wide open and the caption read: *"After all is said and done, there's a lot more said than done!"*

These posters illustrate two great truths about progress or the lack thereof: Ships are not made to stay in harbors – and, talking doesn't make things happen!

Through the years, I gathered additional truths about making progress, including: *"People can't help you get where you are going if they don't know where it is!"*

The point: We must make progress to survive our travels through the jungle because, if we stand still, we will be eaten!

Sometimes, however, an impediment to progress can be our desire to make too much progress too fast.

There will be times when the task either looks – or actually is – so large, or failure appears so likely, it ultimately becomes overwhelming or impossible. We freeze or shut down. That's when the dreaded "I can't do it!" surfaces and we are in real trouble, having lost the most important ingredient of making progress: self-confidence.

The key to real, productive progress is a balance between moving too slowly and charging too quickly.

There are other hindrances to making progress. Let's look at some of them.

I begin with the one hindrance to progress that irritates me most – the popular excuse, "I don't have time." Not *having* time is neither an acceptable reason nor excuse! My rationale is simple. Time is the only resource of which every person on earth has the exact same amount. It is both our most limited resource and our most unforgiving limitation, but we all have the same amount.

No matter who we are or what our station in life may be, we all have exactly the same amount of time – 24 hours, 1,440 minutes, 86,400 seconds – each day. Not more or less. The better excuse, or maybe even a valid reason, is "I did not choose to use my time to do that because ..." Then, you are being honest and accountable to yourself and others.

It is a good practice to view time exactly as you view having a fixed and very limited amount of money.

Ask four "money" questions about how you use your time:

+ Is this necessary?

+ Is it worth the time it costs?

+ Is it the most important thing I should be spending time on?

+ Is it less expensive to have somebody else do it while I do something else?

I have wasted a lot of time and sacrificed a lot of progress by doing things myself, just because I am good at them or simply like doing them. Those things could – and should – have been done by others. If I have time to do them, fine. If doing one of these things impedes progress that I could be making on other things, or others are depending on me to make, that's not fine.

"I forgot!" also is not an acceptable reason or excuse. If you make a list of things you are likely to forget, then you only have to remember two things: where the list is and to look at it. If you carry it somewhere on your person, you only have one thing to remember.

Perhaps the most familiar progress killer is our natural resistance to change. Excuses like *"We've never done it that way before"* and *"That's the way we've always done it"* and *"That's not the way we do it"* emerge from that resistance. When someone says any of these things, he/she's really saying *"We don't want to progress."* Don't waste your time talking to the person who won't change.

General Bert Harbour was a successful leader of the U.S. Air Force Systems Command. Speaking on the value of failures in test programs, Gen. Harbour said, *"There is no need to talk to the person who tells you about today's problems. It's his successor you want to talk to."*

––––––––––––––––

One of the worst enemies of progress is bureaucracy!

Bill Haga was the most unlikely professor at the Naval Postgraduate School. In this very formal, graduate level equivalent to Annapolis, Bill stood out – he looked like a '70s hippie with long hair and casual clothes – but he was a genius.

Bill taught a course titled, The Analysis of Bureaucracy, which is how I acquired three important life-changing lessons, all of which remain very significant to me 30 years later. They all relate to making progress.

The first and most profound of Bill's lessons: ***"Nothing of real significance happens as the result of anything less than a crisis."*** As I continue on my day-to-day safari and observe the jungle around me, I see this to be true, not only in business and politics but also in smaller organizations, churches, communities and the personal lives of many people, including myself.

Tragically, we don't often learn from history, see the obvious outcomes of behavior or "listen to wake-up calls." We don't charge until we are threatened or attacked. We just keep on grazing until a crisis comes that causes a reaction and, almost always, change.

Morris Massey, in his classic video series that began with, "What You Are Is Where You Were When," calls crises in our personal lives Significant Emotional Events.

Massey also says we are "value programmed" almost completely by the time we are 12 years old and permanently by the end of our teen years. Those "programmed" values will not be changed by anything less than a Significant Emotional Event.

The Great Depression, the world wars, the assassinations of President Kennedy and Martin Luther King, Jr. and 9/11/2001 were all Significant Emotional Events for those who witnessed them. 9/11, for example, spurred Washington – and the entire nation – to begin the War on Terror.

The death of a close family member or friend, or being diagnosed with cancer or other serious disease is a Significant Emotional Event.

A drunk driver often doesn't stop driving drunk until after he maims or kills someone. Smokers usually don't stop smoking until they've been diagnosed with emphysema. Hollywood celebrities don't go into rehab until they've been arrested or been involved in a public spectacle.

When a crisis or Significant Emotional Event occurs at any level, things stop and things change. Ultimately, progress is made! Otherwise, the world just plugs along, seeing or not seeing the crisis coming and not doing much about it. Sadly, we rarely make real progress until after a crisis.

I have learned three lessons about crises.

The first is: **If I can pay attention to the factors leading up to a crisis and act beforehand, I'm ahead of the game.** If I know I'm a physical wreck, why wait until I have a heart attack, cancer or a failing skeletal system to exercise, lose weight, quit smoking or drinking alcohol to excess ... whatever?

If I heed the lessons discussed in our chapters on the other three P's, why wait for a crisis to start doing something?

The second crisis lesson is this: **Sometimes you have to create a crisis in order to get anything meaningful accomplished.**

Wow! You mean I need to actually stir things up, intentionally, to get something done? Yes, that's what I mean. You have to create a mini-Significant Emotional Event to awaken the team and move it to action. As the leader, you have to take actions that promote progress. But I've also learned a third lesson along with this one:

If you create a crisis, you or somebody else had better be able to control it. Otherwise, things can get permanently out of control, causing only problems that can never be solved.

Overcome inertia. Determine to make progress before a crisis.

———————————

The second lesson about making progress that Bill Haga taught me was: **"The environment is going to get you!"**

I am not talking about hurricanes and global warming. I am talking about the uncertainty of life. No matter how well I plan, my life is going to be so significantly disrupted at times, I will have to make completely new plans in order to progress.

Sometimes I have to make new plans just to catch up. When I'm attacked, I must first survive. Then, I must lick my wounds and figure out ways to recover. I may have to hide and rest for a while, but if I don't eventually come out of hiding and make progress, I will starve to death – the same fate as if I had been killed.

If I am to survive the jungle, I sometimes need to go back and catch up in order to make progress again, but I have to remain determined if progress can, eventually, be achieved.

A final lesson I learned in post-graduate school about making progress: **"For every organization, there is an appropriate size and formality of its management structure."** One of the biggest hindrances to progress is a management structure that's either too large or too small for the organization.

One of the most important, ongoing tasks of a leader is to adjust the management structure to fit the changing organization. I have seen many organizations of all sizes fail because their leaders did not adjust their structure to the size of their business.

A final key to making progress is having enough confidence in your people to allow decisions to be made by those most knowledgeable and qualified to make that decision. That person isn't always you!

Decide, at the beginning of any task, whether to lead, follow or get out of the way. When you give the most qualified and knowledgeable people a job to do, get out of the way and let them do it.

And remember, people can't help you get where you're going if they don't know where that is. Poor task definition and poor delegation are progress killers. Make sure both you and your team know where you are going and how you are going to get there.

———————

Life in the jungle comes at us fast. We are expected to not only make progress but also to make progress quickly. That's been, generally, a good match for me because I like to go fast, ride roller coasters and do fast things. One thing that kept me up to speed was consistently reading books that related to my career and provided ideas for improved leadership skills.

My daughter Kimberly, another great mentor, is also a "fast" person. She has never been a big reader, so I was very surprised when she gave me a little book by Scott Alexander titled, *Rhinoceros Success*. Since Kimberly gave me that book, I have read it over a dozen times and I remain amazed at how applying its approach affected the remaining years of my career … and my life.

In his little book, Alexander uses the natural characteristics of a rhino to teach many valuable lessons about leading a balanced life. As you might expect, the main message is the rhino's best-known characteristic: It keeps charging, making progress, no matter how much resistance it faces.

Another valuable point also has served me, and others, well. Rhinos have poor eyesight. That's the reason they charge, stop and look, then charge again. We should do the same.

Soon after reading the book, our team developed a motivational campaign for our entire organization based on Rhinoceros Success. During the next five years, we bought and distributed more than 1,000 copies of the book and became known – even at corporate headquarters – as "the rhino people."

By the time I retired, rhino knick-knacks were everywhere, including my office where more than 200 had somehow gathered, given to me by team members, customers and friends.

Truthfully, though, sometimes it's hard to keep charging. Yet, as the laws of the jungle dictate, keep charging or be eaten.

LESSONS:

1. "I didn't have time" and "I forgot" are not good reasons or excuses.

2. The biggest impediment to progress is resistance to change.

3. Nothing of significance happens as a result of anything less than a crisis.

4. The environment is going to get you. Unexpected things will happen, changing plans and impeding progress.

5. There is an appropriate size and formality of management structure for every organization.

6. Keep charging!

TIPS:

1. Change "I didn't have time" to "I did not choose to use my time for that because...."

2. Use a pencil and paper to eliminate the "I forgot" excuse.

3. Don't waste your valuable time with people who don't want to make progress.

4. Overcome inertia. Determine to make progress before a crisis.

5. Expect the unexpected.

6. Define and state tasks well for yourself and your team.

CHAPTER 5

PERFECTION: GOOD ENOUGH IS NOT GOOD ENOUGH

"Anything worth doing is worth doing right."
MY DAD, G.L. LONG, JR.

In today's world of global competition, technology and specialization, customers demand perfection. Perfect cars, products, services. You name it. We all demand it in our personal lives, as well. And, if we don't get perfection, we are not only disappointed, we become angry!

Good enough is not good enough. Things need to be better than good enough. If your customers are angry enough, they act, usually by: 1) returning a defective product and demanding a better one, 2) filing a lawsuit, or 3) moving on to a competitor. And, when things are not good enough in our "other lives," we also take action.

Therefore, if we are providing a product or service, we strive for perfection because we *have* to. We sharpen our claws, perfect our skills and keep fighting. It is, however, easier and more pleasant if we strive for perfection because we also *want* to.

Our attitude about being the best is largely influenced by our attitude about life. Earlier, I told you my dad taught me to do many things. One of them was woodworking. It was his favorite hobby. He had a large workshop behind our garage and he was a master woodworker. He made antique furniture reproductions.

He worked in his shop several hours nearly every night after returning from work and having dinner. I spent many hours in that shop with him – watching, listening and working as his helper ... and I learned. As I got older, I built increasingly more complicated pieces and learned all of the steps in woodworking. It's a unique skill because it has many steps – from cutting the first board to the final finishing and the last coat of polish.

Within all these steps, there are countless opportunities for mistakes and many opportunities for shortcuts and cover-ups. Good enough can be good enough and, when the product is finally finished, nobody is likely to notice. But my dad knew. He noticed!

As we worked on woodworking projects and did other things together, my dad taught me, often saying, *"Anything worth doing is worth doing right. Either do it right or don't do it."*

I've seen him work for hours to correct a mistake and I've seen him start over just because something wasn't right. If he didn't do it right, he didn't do it!

Now, remember – time is our most valuable and unforgiving resource. Anything worth spending it on is worth doing right. Strive for the best because you *want* to.

It is quite natural, having this fatherly mentoring from my boyhood, that I am a perfectionist. My short-term goal in life is: Do everything perfectly every day and enjoy doing it.

The reason for shooting for perfection is simple: When you shoot for perfection, you hit excellence. When you shoot for excellence, you hit good. When you shoot for good, you hit okay and, when you shoot for okay, you hit poor.

Hardly anything ever turns out perfectly, but, if you strive for perfection while keeping it balanced with the other three P's – especially Progress – you will usually get excellence.

The key to having a high-quality organization is the passion for individual perfection.

Wayne Gretzky is regarded as the best ice hockey player who has ever stepped onto the ice. When asked why he was so good, he said, *"Other players skate to where the puck is. I skate to where the puck is going to be."* That meant Gretzky was thinking and plotting every second he was on the ice. He was the predator, stalking the puck and the other players on the ice, not caring where it and they were now as much as where they were going to be next.

To reach the level of excellence that Gretzky reached, you have to work hard but you also have to develop the ability to "skate to where the puck is going to be." That means you have to be thinking all of the time.

Think ahead. Keep moving … and skate to where the puck is going to be. We are given much more mental ability than we ever use and, if we want to achieve excellence, we need to use more of it than others around us.

Learning is both remembering and applying. Understand, your brain is like any muscle in your body. If you exercise your brain, it will remain strong and fit. If you are lazy and use your brain for unchallenging things, your brain will get flabby like your other muscles and eventually deteriorate.

When we quit using our brains, our quest for excellence will stop until we get back into shape … and, believe me, it will be a long and painful process.

In 1972, I was working with a number of other young engineers and managers to produce and deploy our nation's first antiballistic missile system. It was a mammoth undertaking, known first as Sentinel and later as Safeguard. We were headquartered in Huntsville, Alabama.

I was Production Program Manager for the Sprint missile system, consisting of an underground launch tube, control systems and a very, very, very fast short-range missile. It was the predator of missiles, being able to overtake and outrun a rifle bullet in less than two seconds.

Martin Marietta Corporation was building the Sprint system in Orlando, Florida … and I loved that system. It was fast, and I loved the job I had been doing for four years.

Then, one Friday afternoon, while I was in Orlando, we got a phone call with the simple message, "It's over!"

"What's over?" I asked, and it was then I was told the entire system, all of it, had been bargained away as a part of the first Strategic

Arms Limitation Treaty, signed that afternoon between the United States and the U.S.S.R.

I was devastated! Four years of hard but enjoyable work had vanished in an instant.

During the next three years, I did not use my brain. I always had a "job" and got a paycheck, but my assignments required very little mental exercise.

By the time I finally got "a real job" in 1975, I seriously doubted my ability to ever really think, analyze, make good decisions, manage or lead again.

Through a long, slow and difficult process of exercise, I eventually recovered and, after that experience, I was determined to never be in that intellectual condition again. I committed to keep my brain as sharp as I could and to use it the best I could for the rest of my life.

Exercise your brain and keep it strong. You cannot strive for perfection, attempt to balance the Four P's or do much of anything else that's meaningful without it.

One of the secrets to striving for perfection is quickly acknowledging mistakes and starting over.

———————————————

Bill Gates is my hero. It's not because he's one of the richest men on the planet and the biggest elephant in the business jungle. And it's not because he is a great manager and leader, although he is. It's because he has a lot of wisdom about how to navigate and survive in the jungle.

In the July 1995 issue of *US Air Magazine*, there was an interview with him on "The importance of making mistakes." Here's an excerpt:

"Back in 1984, after Microsoft released the version of a spreadsheet called Multiplan for the Apple Macintosh, we discovered a bug that could damage data. When members of the Multiplan team informed me of the problem, they asked if we could send a free corrected version to the product's 20,000 customers. I said yes. There was no argument, no discussion. The answer was obvious.

"Before he left, the team leader said, 'But it is going to cost a lot of money.' It was – almost $250,000.

"Just because it's bad doesn't mean that there is room for discussion," I replied. *"One day you come in to work and lose a quarter of a million dollars. The next day you come in and you try to do better.*

"Apparently people expected a bigger reaction from me, but there was no value in a bigger reaction. There wasn't even any value in spending more than a minute in the meeting. Reacting calmly and constructively to a mistake is not the same as taking it lightly.

"Every employee must understand that management cares about mistakes and is on top of fixing the problems. But setbacks are normal, especially among people and companies trying new things. When employees know that mistakes won't lead to retribution, it creates an atmosphere in which people are willing to come up with ideas and suggest changes. This is important to a company's long-term success. And drawing lessons from mistakes reduces the possibility that errors will be repeated or compounded."

I could have inserted this story in several chapters of this book because it is a perfect example of Balancing the Four P's, all in one short story. It is also an example of superb leadership and a glimpse into why Microsoft and Bill Gates are as successful as they are.

The Air Force's Gen. Harbour points out, *"The success of a test program is failure! If you don't have failures during a test program, there is no need to test an item more than once."*

Let's expand that to acknowledge this: All of life is one big test program. We are going to have failures in our quest for success. If we freeze at the first failure, progress stops. Strive for success but expect failures and learn from them.

The secret is to acknowledge mistakes. Learn from failures. Recover ... and move on.

———————

There is no such thing as having all of the information about anything. If we wait long enough, we can learn more, and even learn something that will change our actions.

Never become a victim of "analysis paralysis" – being afraid to do something because you fear what you do will be wrong.

It is better to do something well that you believed was right but turned out wrong or got criticized for than to do nothing. The laws, policies and procedures will tell you if it is illegal, and your well-developed conscience will tell you if it's immoral.

One of the greatest leadership principles in the jungle states: *"The things that get rewarded are the things that get done!"* If you don't start because you want to make sure you are doing the right thing, nothing will get done. Remember, always keep moving … or be eaten!

LESSONS:

1. Anything worth spending your most precious and limited resource on is worth doing right.

2. You usually get at least one level of quality below what you expect.

3. Your brain is like a muscle. If you don't use it, you lose it.

4. Life is a test program in which there will be both failure and success.

5. You will never have all of the information on anything. Start anyway.

TIPS:

1. Strive for perfection because you *want* to.

2. Think ahead. Skate to where the puck is going to be.

3. Exercise your brain and keep it sharp.

4. Acknowledge mistakes, learn from failures, recover, and move on quickly.

5. Don't succumb to "analysis paralysis."

CHAPTER 6

PULLING TOGETHER: THERE ARE NO JUSTA'S

People don't care how much you know
when they know how much you care.

This is one of the most difficult parts of the safari, but the lessons learned are some of the most significant because they are about relationships with others.

While Progress, Perfection and Positive Attitude are complex and important, Pulling Together with others is critical to our success and happiness in all aspects of our lives. It is in this area that I have learned many lessons, some the hard way and some very late.

I begin with the most difficult, most disappointing, but most important lesson I learned about Pulling Together.

Unless you are very fortunate or just plain lucky, there is at least one member of every team who simply does not want to Pull

Together – to cooperate with you or the others, to get along or play on the team. It's just not on their agenda. They love slowing things down, getting attention, causing trouble and they never have a positive attitude … at least about things that are important to your team.

These individuals come in all sizes, colors, shapes and positions – some above you, some beside you and some below you. Sometimes you can get rid of them and sometimes you just have to live with them, but to ignore them is very dangerous.

They make all aspects of Balancing the Four P's incredibly more difficult, and you will have to do the best you can until one of you leaves, dies or changes. Sometimes the probability of leaving or dying is greater than changing because they usually are dug in.

But, no matter their station, never ignore these dangerous animals or underestimate their power. Sorry, that's life. To overcome these powerful predators, let's look at what the rest of the team can do to help pull together despite these spoilers.

A good team uses every willing member's talents. There are no "little people" nor "justa's," as in "I'm justa _____." Every person on a good team has a role as important as – but different from – the roles of the others. Each contributes to the team's success or becomes part of its failure.

Over the long term, the employees you might be tempted to consider "justa's" usually have a tremendous impact on the team's and on your personal success or failure. Treating all members of the team with consideration, respect and kindness is paramount. Why? Because big elephants and little scorpions have one thing in common. They can both kill you. Bottom line: People are much more likely to pull together when they are treated like people.

John Kleban taught me that leaders can give away authority but can never give away responsibility. With this truth in mind, a leader must walk a relatively fine line between getting too close to those around him and not knowing them well enough.

In life's jungle, if the pack leader strays on one side of the line, he becomes a buddy and loses both his objectivity and the respect of the herd. If he strays to the other side, he is perceived as aloof and uncaring and he loses the others' loyalty.

With that word of caution, it is the leader's responsibility to get to know the other members of the team, respect them, protect them and care about them. People don't care how much you know about them when they know how much you care about them.

For many years, a poster in my office showed tiny and defenseless white birds sitting on the back of a huge rhino. The caption was, "*Familiarity Breeds Confidence.*"

Both the birds and the rhino know which is which. But, the birds and the rhino are familiar with each other and they understand each has a role in the relationship. The birds are not particularly worried about predators as long as they are on the rhino's back ... and the rhino is not worried about having annoying bugs feasting on its back as long as the birds are there.

So how does this work when you have to do unpleasant tasks?

Admittedly, it's a lot simpler when things are going well, but the same principles apply in bad times. As with seeking perfection, it's all in our approach.

When people believe you respect and care about them, they react entirely differently to unpleasant actions than when they believe you see them as, simply, a number instead of as individuals.

During the times we were closing plants and laying people off, we tried to treat those affected like we would want to be treated under the same circumstances. We informed them early, explained why the actions were being taken, kept them updated and provided support and help throughout the process.

Does that mean they liked it? Does that mean nobody disliked the company or me, personally? Does that mean there were no threats or sabotage? The answer to all these is "No."

I've already admitted the mistake I made in assuming – just because we were being humane – all the surviving employees liked me. That was being gullible. But I will tell you, the vast majority of those adversely affected pulled together and delivered good products and services until their last day.

Pulling Together is about teamwork and good team members covering for each other. When one is down or weak, the others pull harder.

The concept of dividing responsibility and accountability equally among members of an effective team is as foreign as it is to the partners in a good marriage. Nothing is ever 50/50! If two people are trying to divide the tasks 50/50, there is a probability that something will not get done or will be done poorly.

On the other hand, if both are working toward dividing the tasks 75/75 or even 100/100, the overlap will take them effectively toward their goal.

I believe that this document in my "Lessons Learned" archives was originally written by advice columnist Ann Landers. I think this advice is timeless.

THE 10 COMMANDMENTS OF HOW TO GET ALONG WITH PEOPLE

1. Keep skid chains on your tongue: Always say less than you think. Cultivate a low, calm and persuasive voice. How you say it often counts more than what you say.

2. Make promises sparingly and keep them faithfully, no matter what it costs you.

3. Never let an opportunity pass to say a kind and encouraging thing to or about somebody. Praise good work done, regardless of who did it. If criticism is needed, criticize helpfully – not spitefully.

4. Be interested in others. Rejoice with those who rejoice. Mourn with those who weep. Let everyone you meet, however humble, know you regard him/her as important.

5. Be cheerful. Keep the corners of your mouth turned up. Hide your pains, worries and disappointments under a smile. Laugh at good clean stories and learn to tell them.

6. Preserve an open mind on all debatable questions. Discuss but don't argue. It is a mark of superior minds to disagree, but in a friendly way.

7. Let your virtues speak for themselves and refuse to talk of other's vices. Discourage gossip. Make a rule to say nothing of another unless it is something good.

8. Be careful of another's feelings. Wit and humor at another's expense is rarely worth the effort – and may come back to haunt you when you least expect it.

9. Pay no attention to ill-natured remarks about you. Simply live so that nobody will believe them.

10. Don't be too anxious about what is due you. Do your work, be patient, keep your disposition nice, forget self and you will have your best chance of being rewarded.

I end this chapter where I started.

Pulling Together is difficult, even in good times. It's even more difficult in hard times and it's becoming almost a lost art. In our warp-speed trips through jungles, it's every animal for him/herself. Eat or be eaten. Kill or be killed.

However, each of us, regardless of our position, has to live and work with the other inhabitants of the jungle, even if only for a relatively brief time. Those who develop the ability to quickly pull together with the other animals, regardless of how long they are in that jungle, are the ones most likely to survive and even thrive. That's our goal!

LESSONS:

1. Some people refuse to pull together, and those people are dangerous.

2. There are no "little people" or "justa's" on a good team.

3. A leader can give away authority but not responsibility.

4. Even in unpleasant times, people react according to how they are treated.

5. 100/100 works better than 50/50.

TIPS:

1. Don't allow those who will not pull together to change your course or stop your progress.

2. Treat no one as a "justa."

3. Stay within the boundaries of your position.

4. Get to know, care about and respect other team members.

5. Give your 100 percent willingly.

6. Pay attention to the Ten Commandments of How to Get Along With People.

7. Criticize behaviors, not people.

CHAPTER 7

POSITIVE ATTITUDE: WHETHER QUARTERS OR MILLIONS

*"It's not what you'd do with millions if millions
should ever be your lot — it's what you're doing today
with the dollar and a quarter you've got."*
UNKNOWN

A young woman went to her mother and told her about how things were so hard in her life. She did not know how she was going to make it and she wanted to give up. She was tired of fighting and struggling. It seemed that as soon as one problem was solved, a new one arose.

Her mother took her to the kitchen. She filled three pots with water. In the first, she put carrots; in the second, she put eggs; and, in the third, she put coffee.

She let them sit and boil without saying a word. In about 20 minutes, she turned off the burners. She fished the carrots out and placed them in a bowl. She pulled the eggs out and placed them in a bowl. Then she ladled the coffee out and placed it in a cup. Turning to the daughter, she asked, "Tell me what you see?"

"Carrots, eggs and coffee," the girl replied, looking puzzled.

Her mother brought her closer and asked her to feel the carrots. She did and noted they were soft. She then asked her to take an egg and break it. After pulling off the shell, she observed the hard-boiled egg. Finally, the mom asked her to sip the coffee. The daughter smiled as she tasted the steaming liquid and smelled its rich aroma.

Each of these objects, her mother explained, had faced the same adversity – boiling water – but each reacted differently. The carrot went in strong, hard and unrelenting. However, after being subjected to the boiling water, it softened and became weak. The egg had been fragile. Its thin outer shell had protected its liquid interior. But, after sitting through the boiling water, its inside became hardened. The ground coffee beans were unique, however. After they were in the boiling water for a brief time, they had changed the water.

"Which are you?" the mom asked her daughter. "When adversity knocks on your door, how do you respond? Are you a carrot, an egg or coffee?"

Which am I? Am I the carrot that seems strong, but with pain and adversity, do I wilt and become soft and lose my strength?

Ask yourself, "Am I the egg that starts out with a malleable spirit, but changes with the heat? Did I have a fluid spirit but, after a death, a financial hardship, or some other trial, I became hardened? Does my shell look the same but, on the inside, am I bitter and tough with a stiff spirit and a hardened heart? Or, am I like the coffee bean?"

The coffee bean actually changes the hot water, the very circumstance that brings the pain. When the water gets hot, the brown beans release their fragrance and flavor. If I am like the bean, when things are at their worst, I get better and change the situation around me. When the *hours are the darkest and trials are their greatest, do I elevate to another level?*

This recent parable of unknown origin tells us that we should work at being coffee instead of a carrot or an egg.

Tim Porter, my son-in-law, has been my strongest supporter in writing this book. Tim is also a good guide as we travel through the jungle because he brings me new, fresh ideas from the perspective of a young lion. We spend hours discussing life in the various jungles we encounter.

One of Tim's favorite sayings is, "Don't let your circumstances determine your actions. Make your actions determine your circumstances!" Another is, "Never underestimate the importance of being where you are now!"

Both the mother in the carrot, egg and coffee story and Tim realize that *attitude determines altitude.* How high you fly depends on your attitude about the flight. You can make a difference in your life, today, and in the lives of others if you have a positive attitude. *Make your actions determine your circumstances* and take advantage of those circumstances today.

Earlier, I said I admire Bill Gates for many things but, most of all, for his practical and positive attitude about life. During a speech to high school students, he gave them 11 excellent rules about the real world.

Rule One was something my dad taught me early in my life. I started sharing this same rule with my two daughters from the time they were able to understand: *Life is not fair!*

Bummer! It is within that life context that we are challenged to maintain a positive attitude and – let's face it – that's sometimes very hard to do. But, if we are going to be content, successful and have a seamless life, we must also be wise enough to realize, many days we are going up against tough odds. Realizing and accepting that life is not fair helps prepare us to meet that challenge. Accept that life is not fair and don't expect it to be. Keep a positive attitude anyway. If you can't enjoy what you're doing most of the time, do something else.

———————————

As leaders, our attitude is even more important because we not only set our attitude each day but also the environment for many around us. I learned, rather quickly, when I had "the corner office," the way I behaved each morning on the way to that office set the mood of the entire herd. I learned it was essential to walk confidently, have a smile and, when greeted, say either, *"I'm having a great day!"* or *"I'm having a good time!"* So, I did that, even if I didn't feel like smiling or was not having a great day or a good time.

Sometimes you simply have to "fake it until you make it." You have to enjoy what you are doing or act like you do until you do. This has two advantages – it makes others feel better and it also makes you feel better – because you eventually believe yourself.

But what if you think things are so bad or a situation has lasted so long, you can't fake it anymore? Try going to an airport, a hospital or a large store and observe all those less fortunate than you. Then go home, count your blessings and get back to work.

If that doesn't help brighten your outlook, have the courage to make changes in your life that will bring back your lost positive attitude.

We can spend our lives waiting for more money, more time, more talent – waiting for our lives to get better. But, instead of waiting, be thankful for what we have and use that gratitude to make a real difference – in the lives of others.

In 1995, our company had been through some very rough waters but had weathered the storms with enough success that I was asked to speak to a large group about how we were achieving our successes.

After many hours of consideration, I realized our secret ingredient was our team's positive attitude. So, much to the surprise of many, including the Chief Operations Officer who had invited me, my presentation was titled, *"Attitude is Everything!"*

After briefly explaining some of the problems we had faced and how we approached their solutions, I turned to the basic message. Using the popular Dave Letterman Top Ten format, I presented the Top Ten List of Questions for Attitude Self-Evaluation. I am convinced the list has stood the test of time, so here it is:

THE TOP 10 LIST OF QUESTIONS
FOR ATTITUDE SELF-EVALUATION

#10: Can I admit I made a mistake?

#9: Do I really listen to others?

#8: Am I more interested in fixing the problem than fixing the blame?

#7: Am I part of the solution and not part of the problem?

#6: Do I treat others the way I want to be treated?

#5: Do I follow as well as I lead?

#4: Do I give others the proper credit?

#3: Do I have confidence in myself and in others?

#2: Do I work at Balancing the Four P's?

#1: Do I "Do what's right?"

If you can honestly give positive answers to each of these questions, you will have a positive attitude. Why? Because you will feel good about yourself, and most of the animals around you will feel good having you in their herd.

Work on answering, "Yes" to all the Attitude Self-Evaluation questions.

When positive attitudes are lost and friction or anger develops among members of the team, Progress, Perfection and Pulling Together suffer immediately.

I saw the effects of this and began learning lessons about it from an early age. I am indebted to my mother for many things, including providing me a firm spiritual foundation. But my mom had a bad temper and held grudges.

My dad, on the other hand, angered slowly and forgot grievances more quickly. Out of this situation came one of his most profound statements. When my mother would get angry, which she did frequently and for long periods, my dad would simply say, *"You have two choices: You can either get happy or die mad."*

When you think about it, those are the only two choices we all have when we become dissatisfied or angry – we can get happy or die mad! The preferable choice? Doing what it takes without jeopardizing principles to re-establish happiness.

Choose to get happy rather than to die mad.

One of my most often-quoted rhymes is, "It's not what you'd do with millions if millions should ever be your lot, it's what you're doing today with the dollar and a quarter you've got." We can use the "dollar and a quarter" we have rather than waiting for the millions we may never have.

So, whether you have five quarters or five million dollars, have a positive attitude and use your talents and resources to make a difference in your organization and in the world.

LESSONS:

1. When faced with adversity, we can become a carrot, an egg or a coffee bean.

2. Our attitude determines our altitude and affects the attitude of those around us.

3. Life is not fair. Don't expect it to be.

4. The Attitude Self-Evaluation is a valuable tool for developing a positive attitude.

5. When we are dissatisfied or angry, we have only two choices: Get happy or die mad.

TIPS:

1. Work at being coffee instead of a carrot or an egg.

2. Make your actions determine your circumstances, and take advantage of those circumstances today.

3. Accept that life is not fair. Keep a positive attitude anyway.

4. If you can't enjoy what you are doing most of the time, do something else.

5. Sometimes you have to "fake it until you make it" to regain a positive attitude.

6. Work at answering "Yes" to all of the Attitude Self-Evaluation questions.

7. Choose to get happy rather than to die mad.

CHAPTER 8

THE CHANGING LAWS
OF THE JUNGLE

*"What's popular is not always right,
and what's right is not always popular!"*

The original title of this chapter was, simply, "Do What's Right!" However, as I began to write, I realized there is no definition in the English language that is more controversial and open to debate in today's jungle than that of *"doing what's right."*

Regardless of what I say about "What's Right," many will disagree. Some will be offended and others will be angry. So, I started to not write this chapter at all. However, those who know me well and have been my guides through the jungles would be shocked and disappointed if I had not at least tried to address the changing laws we attempt to live with today.

For years, I told those whom I led to "Do What's Right," never doubting for a minute they would know exactly what I meant.

Many of us even wore big lapel buttons that read, "Do What's Right!" It may have been naive of me to believe those on my team knew exactly what that meant, but I don't think so. I think most knew what was right.

We learned on September 11, 2001, that not everybody defines "Do What's Right" the same. But, life is uncertain, and improving your life and the lives of others is important!

The first time I realized how fragile life really is was on the island of Guam in 1965. Guam is a 30-mile-long island that was essentially uninhabited back then, except for a huge U.S. Navy base on one end, the tiny town of Agana in the middle and the huge Andersen U.S. Air Force base at the other end.

The Vietnam War was in full swing, and I was a U.S. Army Ordnance Technical Operations Officer. That long title meant I worked on bombs.

My task on Guam was to help recondition defective bombs built in U.S. Army ammunition plants for use by the Air Force and Navy. They were tricky little rascals, so tricky, in fact, that even the Explosive Ordnance Disposal guys didn't like to work with them.

One day I was in a bunker at Andersen Air Force Base with a big guy from Alabama who was known for his impulsive nature. He was working on one side of the concrete bunker and I on the other when I heard the dreaded sound of a baseball-size bomb arming. We were in a room full of them! When I walked over to him, he said, "I can just push this plate back up and everything will be okay, right?"

It was the detonating plate! If he had pushed it without asking, we would have been vaporized. It would have all been over. Instead, I disarmed the bomb and we escaped, unhurt.

That night, I realized, more than ever before, life is very uncertain and doing what's right is important. It's an unsettling realization, but I concluded that I must be ready to die at any moment. I also decided I needed to reaffirm what "Do What's Right" means.

Don't assume you will be guaranteed a certain number of years to live and make a difference. There are no guarantees.

Your actions will ultimately be based on your belief structure. That is your personal foundation. Your path and your guides through the jungle may be different from mine, but I encourage you to make sure they are positive ones aimed at improving your life and the lives of others.

However, the fact that you think you are doing what's right does not make it right. You may have chosen to misinterpret or even ignore the good and valid basis of your belief structure. You may know what's right and yet choose to do something entirely different.

On the other hand, you may have to redefine what's right based on your continual study of the source of your beliefs and your sincere search for improvement. That does not make the source of your belief wrong. It makes your belief or action wrong, and only you can change it!

Continually assess your actions against your personal values to make sure they match. If they don't, change the actions and not the foundation.

Here's an illustration from my life:

> I returned to Guam in 1966 when I encountered the biggest challenge to my personal values. I had a Significant Emotional Event one summer afternoon that led to my learning several of my most important lessons about "doing what's right." It was there and then that I met my first African-American friend. I was a white Army lieutenant and Aaron Cobb was a black Air Force lieutenant. We had worked together, day and night, for several weeks on Guam and were friendly but not friends.

> One Sunday afternoon, I went to sleep under the equatorial sun and became badly sunburned, a court martial offense for military personnel on Guam. I was now a very red and hurting white Army lieutcnant!

> Aaron took care of me for four days while I secretly recovered to avoid both charges and further embarrassment. He brought me food and Solarcaine and did my job for me until I recovered. He quickly became my friend with his many acts of kindness and unselfish attention … and it was from that experience and friendship I began to learn how wrong I had been about prejudice and discrimination.

I could attribute my error to my value programming and spending the first 24 years of my life in a very narrow segment of society, but I was still wrong.

It is not "doing what's right" to be prejudiced or discriminate against any other person for something they cannot change! It's that simple. I cannot change my height, my past, or the color of my skin – so don't treat me differently because of them.

And don't prejudge – the root word of prejudice. Assess the people around you based on how they behave, contribute and perform, not by things they cannot change.

Open, honest communication is as critical to doing what's right as it is to Balancing the Four P's.

Let's assume, for a moment, the dream situation where you are a member of a team and all the team members share your view of what's right. All are sincerely trying to do the right thing and balance the Four P's.

Even under ideal conditions – and certainly in the real world – what each person considers to be the right thing may be different, based on the amount and accuracy of knowledge and information he/she may have. Then each, independently, does what he/she thinks is right. However, things turn out all wrong.

As a result, each then accuses the others of not doing what was right. The situation becomes a mess, only because not all were on the same page when the task began or actions were taken. The right thing for a leader to do in these situations of conflict is to make sure everyone has all of the information needed to do the job.

If conflicts still exist, be careful not to judge and accuse before you get the facts. First, go to the person or people you think caused a problem or did the wrong thing and get their side of a story. Sort out the facts and handle the misunderstanding – head on and quickly – lest it develops into an irreparable situation. It's much easier to prevent a problem than it is to fix one.

It would be a much simpler world if we all agreed on what's right ... and you all agreed with me! However, we do not live in a world where most people agree on what it means to do what's right.

In fact, at least five definitions of "what's right" have become prominent in the United States. The first is a well-publicized corporate view – "right" is whatever increases the bottom line and you can get away with doing.

The second view is "situational ethics," in which "right" is not concrete but is fluid and changing, depending on the surrounding circumstances.

The third view is that there are no definite rights or wrongs. Anything is "right" if you like it and it makes you feel good – the "if it feels good, do it" philosophy.

The fourth view defines "right" both by laws of man and by the religious laws on which our country was founded. While the majority of people in the U.S. subscribe to this belief, that majority is dwindling rapidly.

There also is a fifth and very sobering view of what's right that has become apparent in our world since 9/11. This view of "right" differs sharply on the subject of "doing what's right." For the rapidly growing number of people who hold this belief, "doing what's right" is defined as hating and killing Americans, and these people defend their belief to the death. To make matters more complicated, they claim to be friendly until they act.

As we travel through our lives of work, neighborhood, social interaction, sports – all of them – we can no longer assume that everybody defines "doing what's right" the same way we do.

In order to communicate and be successful in Balancing the Four P's, we have to learn how others define "doing what's right." We have to know who is in our jungle and then seek ways to Balance the Four P's as we live alongside them without violating our principles or killing each other.

Take the time to listen and understand what others believe without assuming they agree with you. Decide what your values are and stick to them. What's popular is not always right, and what's right is not always popular.

LESSONS:

1. I must be ready to die at any moment ... because I might.

2. Just because you think what you are doing is right does not make it right.

3. Prejudice and discrimination – based on things another cannot change – are wrong.

4. You can no longer assume everybody defines "doing what's right" the same way you do.

TIPS:

1. Continually assess your actions against your values. If they don't match, change your actions.

2. Assess people based on how they behave, contribute and perform.

3. Fix problems quickly, based on facts, and move on.

4. Decide what your principles are and stick to them.

5. Learn what others believe before assuming they agree with you.

CHAPTER 9

AT THE HEAD OF THE PACK

"I am not an extraordinary man.
I am an ordinary man who is extraordinarily motivated."
TEDDY ROOSEVELT

In Chapter One, I mentioned I would rather lead than follow. Here's why: Being at the head of the pack, you have a vast view of the landscape and can choose the direction the pack will take. However, the challenge of being at the head of the pack brings with it the responsibility for those following behind you.

When you're at the head of the pack – and you want to make continual progress – it's your responsibility to bring everyone on your team up-to-speed. It's also your responsibility to help them work as an efficient and effective team.

John Kleban, who was at the head of my pack for 10 years, never appeared to be very interested in the on-the-job training of his staff. He seemed to assume you knew how to do your job and, if you didn't, you could learn on your own. Therefore, when he appeared at a staff meeting with copies of a one-page essay for each of us titled, "The Winners Are Still Winning," we were all surprised.

There was nothing to indicate the essay's origin. He had obviously extracted it from somewhere. There was a paragraph on each of the following seven statements:

+ Winners depend on themselves.

+ Winners recognize the importance of other people.

+ Winners look for solutions, not scapegoats.

+ Winners are less concerned with image than with accomplishment.

+ Winners act on their own authority.

+ Winners are tenacious in the pursuit of their goals.

+ The winner's goal is the accomplishment, not the reward.

I have read that essay countless times and find it to be as valuable today as it was then. In observing John for a decade, it was apparent to me that, as good and confident as he was, he was constantly in the process of on-the-job training in a quest for self-improvement.

My guess? He probably read this list often and worked at making course corrections. If he needed to do that, then I – in my leadership role – certainly did, too.

Never stop your on-the-job training and your quest for self-improvement.

As you're traveling through life's jungle, it can be easy to confuse your position on the organizational chart with your leadership skills. You may think, because of your position, you are a great leader while others perceive you as just an overpaid administrator. You may think you are a lion or rhino in life's jungle, while others see you as a water buffalo, a monkey or worst of all, just prey to be eaten … roadkill.

The differences in these perceptions – remember perceptions are reality to their owners – lead to corresponding differences in many other areas, including the quality of the results.

People follow leaders because they want to. People follow managers because they have to and they don't follow administrators at all, even though they may pretend to. Instead, they covertly follow the manager or leader above the administrator or simply do whatever they think is best … and then hope for a good outcome.

What is the key part of the critical process? It is getting our perceptions of ourselves to match our reality and to learn, honestly, whether we are perceived as a leader, manager or administrator. The results can be surprising because it is possible to be pleasantly surprised as well as supremely disappointed.

I have known many administrators and managers who are perceived as, and treated like, leaders. When you are one of those fortunate ones, you are a valuable asset and may be in a position to play a key role in important tasks.

Use your BEST Team (Buddies who Ensure Success and Truth) to learn what type of leadership animal you really are.

How well we function as a leader is influenced by the nature of the task and our ability to get it performed. There are some skills each of us is good at and some things we are not.

My dad taught me plumbing, electrical and woodworking, and I'm pretty good at them. Therefore, I know how to lead people who are doing those tasks. A bricklayer I am not – terrible at it – so I am not qualified to lead bricklayers.

I was once told, *"It's okay to have your air castles, but make sure they are built on concrete foundations."*

When you are asked to lead something you know you cannot do, it is better to say so at the beginning than to fail and let others down in the process.

Don't try to lead people doing something you don't know how to do yourself.

On the other hand, there is much to be gained from taking on a task that you know you can do but others don't think you can do. John Kleban once advised me to always try to get assigned tasks involving things that were broken rather than things that were in good shape. His wisdom was simple – if you fix something that's broken, you are a hero. If you start with something that's in good shape, you will either not be noticed or you will break it and get only negative attention.

Don't be hesitant to take on a task you know you can do.

Be prepared to take responsibility, give the credit or take the blame – and do all three quickly. If you cannot take responsibility, avoid getting into a leadership position. When you give credit, you build valuable capital and gain respect. When you quickly take the blame you deserve, you save time and also gain respect.

Here's a twist! When you take the blame, even if you don't think it is yours – and if taking the blame isn't going to permanently damage you – you save time and energy ... and you may get valuable points for doing so.

Most of the time people are not going to move on until blame has been placed. Once blame has been assigned, they see closure and are then ready to move on.

A simple, "If you are looking for somebody to blame, blame me," will be so shocking and refreshing, you actually get points for it. When the rest of the herd realizes how much time was being wasted trying to find which animal to blame, they want to just drop it. And, sometimes, you can even remind them, once the blame is fixed, the problem still has to be solved.

Here's an example from my jungle journey:

When I moved to the Textron Corporate Headquarters as a Group Vice President, Jim Hardymon was CEO and Chairman of the Board. He was the biggest lion in all the jungle. But Jim did not sleep like most lions. Most who knew him thought he never slept at all.

Jim worked hard, studied hard and was always at the top of his game ... and, Jim loved details. He carried a huge briefcase everywhere he went and he had you in it! He knew more about all of us than we knew about ourselves.

One more thing: Jim had a ferocious temper! Shortly after I arrived at Textron's headquarters, I attended a meeting with Jim, his staff and my peers … and it didn't take too long before things were going downhill rapidly. When that happened, Jim became angry.

When he got into that mode, the careers of one or more of our team members was likely to end instantly. In his anger, he asked, "Who's going to take responsibility for this mess and do something about it?" I took a calculated risk and said I would.

The others in the room looked incredulous. But, Jim calmed down, thanked me and it was over. I did the job for him and I believe that first encounter helped me later in my career, when I really needed him in my corner. I don't think he ever forgot that afternoon … and I know I haven't.

What is the moral of this story? Give the credit and take the blame if it is not going to get you killed. It saves time and energy.

––––––––––––

There's nothing wrong with being better than others. It's acting better than others that's wrong. If you don't think you are the best person to lead, then don't try to be the leader. If you are the best person and are selected to lead, then prove you are the best by the job you do. Remember, winners are less concerned with image than with accomplishment.

––––––––––––

Good leaders are also good followers. Be prepared to temporarily follow or get out of the way, even if you are the leader.

———————

Good leaders are decisive. Baseball great Yogi Berra was famous for having many wise and humorous sayings. One was, "When you come to a fork in the road, take it."

In reality, when you come to a fork in the road, you have three choices: You can take one of the two paths, you can sit down or you can turn around in confusion and go back.

As a leader, it is much better to start down the path you consider best and remain ready for it to turn than to sit down or go back. Be decisive.

———————

Good leaders take care of their people and expect the best performance from them. The introduction to Donald Trump's popular TV show, *The Apprentice*, says, "It's not personal – it's business!" Be careful with that if you are leading people. Those being led can easily mistake business for personal, especially when being criticized.

My dad told me, "You can get more flies with honey than with vinegar." It is generally easier to take a positive, constructive approach to problems because, bottom line, people will live down to your expectations, especially if you don't have any expectations.

Always make certain you criticize behaviors rather than people.

———————

In the stage play, *Annie*, Daddy Warbucks brags, "There's no reason to be nice to people on the way up if you are never coming down!" In reality, it's the very fortunate leader who never comes down at some point, even if only temporarily.

Therefore, it is best to be nice to all those around you on the ladder – regardless of your current position on the organizational chart – lest those below you pull that ladder out from under you. Over the long term, the little animals in the jungle determine your eventual success or failure as much as the big animals.

Be nice on your way up. You may come down the same ladder.

———————————

Finally, recognize your responsibility as a leader to stay in control of both whom you lead and whom you allow to lead you. While not always the case, a good rule of thumb is: If you are paying, you are leading!

Your employer and its representatives above you pay you, so they are entitled to your best service, courtesy and respect. You lead those whom you pay, including not only your employees in your business jungle but those in your other jungles as well. The list includes doctors, dentists, lawyers, painters, plumbers and hosts/hostesses in restaurants.

Some individuals you'll meet on your treks through the jungles have a hard time with this concept. Treat them with courtesy and respect and expect them to provide their best service, along with their courtesy and respect … but be wary! Don't let them treat you as if they are paying you by providing inferior service or stealing your most valuable resource: time.

If you cannot, willingly and happily, follow those who are paying you, make a change. And, if you are not getting good service, respect and courteous treatment from those you are paying, make a change ... and regain control.

Give respect and good service to those who pay you and demand respect and good service from those you are paying.

LESSONS

1. Good leaders never stop learning and improving.

2. Your success as a leader depends on others' perception of you, the nature of the task and your ability to do it.

3. When you take responsibility quickly, you build valuable capital and gain respect.

4. When you take blame that doesn't permanently hurt you, you save time and energy ... and it may get you valuable points.

5. People live both up and down to your expectations.

TIPS:

1. Never stop your on-the-job training and your quest for self-improvement.

2. Give the credit and take the blame … if it is not going to get you killed. It saves time and energy.

3. Criticize the behavior, not the person, unless the person deserves the criticism.

4. Be nice on your way up. You may come down the same ladder.

5. Give respect and good service to those who pay you, and demand respect and good service from those you are paying.

CHAPTER 10

HORSES IN THE JUNGLE?

"When the horse is dead, get off!"
UNKNOWN

I don't care much for horses. They are bigger and stronger than I am, and we both know it. They take advantage of me and I don't like that. Fortunately, we rarely meet a horse in a jungle for one simple reason: They don't last long there!

That being said, three of my best lessons come from sayings and stories involving horses … so I give credit to the critters, although I don't want to be very close to one and definitely will avoid riding one.

There is a sign over the cash register in Fallen's Barbeque Restaurant in Thomasville, Georgia, which reads, "When the horse is dead, get off!"

It means, simply, when something is over, let it go and move on. This can apply not only to dead horses but also to situations, relationships and mistakes.

I have spent many hours in my life worrying about or trying to resuscitate dead horses. Neither ever accomplished anything. You cannot resuscitate a dead horse!

A simple essay with a similar message is titled, "A Reason, A Season, A Lifetime," written by Brian A. "Drew" Chalker, and I have used it in many of my treks through the jungles.

> *"People come into your life for a reason, a season or a lifetime. When you figure out which it is, you know exactly what to do.*
>
> *When someone is in your life for a reason, it is usually to meet a need you have expressed outwardly or inwardly. They have come to assist you through a difficulty, to provide you with guidance and support, to aid you physically, emotionally, or spiritually. They may seem like a Godsend, and they are. They are there for the reason you need them to be.*
>
> *Then, without any wrongdoing on your part, this person will say or do something to bring the relationship to an end. Sometimes they die. Sometimes they walk away. Sometimes they act up or out and force you to take a stand. What we must realize is that our need is met, our desire fulfilled; their work is done. The prayer you sent up has been answered and it is now time to move on.*
>
> *When people come into your life for a season, it is because your turn has come to share, grow, or learn. They bring you an experience of peace or make you laugh. They may teach you something you have never done. They usually give you an unbelievable amount of joy.*

Believe it! It is real, but only for a season. Then, they too are gone.

Lifetime relationships teach you lifetime lessons, those things you must build upon in order to have a solid emotional foundation. Your job is to accept the lesson, love the person/people anyway and put what you have learned to use in all other relationships and areas of your life."

Sometimes we believe a relationship is for a lifetime when it is only for a reason or season.

In 2005, as I was moving from a neighborhood, I met Bob. Bob and I became fast friends. We e-mailed regularly, talked daily, met for breakfast every week and visited often. We had a lot in common and we enjoyed each other's company. We taught each other many things. Bob and his wife prepared meals for us every night one time when Carole was ill. Ours had all the appearances of a close and lasting friendship.

Then we spent an entire week together and things did not go as well as we had planned. Suddenly, without a warning, a fight or a "goodbye," it was over. We both knew it, and we both let it go.

What we had thought was a lifetime friendship was only for a season. But what good times we had during that season!

Several years ago, I was in a situation where the horse was dead but we continued to try to ride it. Somebody in the group said, "We are playing to just get tired!" That statement hit me like a rock, and it has stuck with me ever since.

It's another way of effectively making this same point. When what you are doing is only making you and others tired and is leading nowhere productive, stop wasting your time continuing to do it.

When the horse or the relationship, the situation or the mistake is dead, let it go and move on. **Don't play to just get tired.**

My second horse story developed over many years of my life.

When I was about 20 years old, somebody told me, "You can lead a horse to water but you can't make it drink." When I was about 40, somebody else told me that wasn't true. They said, "You can lead a horse to water and you can make it drink if you put salt in its oats."

I based much of my leadership career on this wise principle. But, it was not until I was 57 years old and retired that I learned, on my own, the final and key phrase in this horse story – "You can lead a horse to water and you can make it drink, *but you can never change the kind of horse it is.*" I wish I had known the end at the beginning – life would have been much simpler and many outcomes would have been less disappointing.

Only then did I realize that, throughout my career, I had spent a lot of time and effort trying to change plow horses into thoroughbreds. You can never do that. All you end up with are plow horses that are not thirsty!

My lesson was learned too late. Both thoroughbreds and plow horses have their place. Don't try to win races with plow horses and don't plow fields with thoroughbreds. Neither effort will result in a successful outcome.

On many occasions during the last nine years of my career, I inherited teams and team members I was given to restructure. I assumed each of them had the capability and the desire to be a thoroughbred. In some cases, it took me only minutes, hours or days to learn what kind of horses they really were. In other cases, it took longer, and for some, I never learned. Instead, I rode them until they failed or somebody shot them.

It would have been much smarter for me, and much kinder for the horses, if I had not been so gullible. They were happy being plow horses and I should have let them remain plow horses.

Work hard to assess whether you have a real thoroughbred on your team or just a really likable plow horse.

My third lesson involving a horse was also one I never implemented well! It comes from the saying, "Stay in the middle of the posse and low in the saddle!"

When you are in a new and unfamiliar situation, a new organization or with a new herd, take time to learn before you speak and act. There are appropriate times to lead, appropriate times to follow and appropriate times to get out of the way. There are appropriate times to speak and appropriate times to be quiet and listen.

It is generally smarter and safer to take time to determine what's appropriate in that situation. But, again, I nearly always thought I needed to be the one to be out front and I frequently either got shot at or actually got shot from the back, side or front. Fortunately, I never died – but sometimes the wounds were deep and the recovery period long.

My most memorable example of my failure to heed this advice comes not from my professional jungle but from one of my church jungles. Yes, churches are jungles, too!

Four young people had been hired to become missionaries. The church leaders held a seminar one Saturday to educate the members on how to support these missionaries. Shortly thereafter, a call went out for somebody to facilitate the departure and transition of the missionaries and to make sure the many things that needed to be done got done.

Carole and I volunteered, knowing there were several potential dangers in doing so. There were lions – church leaders who insisted on having their way and needing to exercise their authority. There were hyenas that made a lot of noise when things did not go their way. There were wolves that ran in packs and liked to attack and pile on. But, believing we had the credentials and time, and that we could be of service to the church, the missionaries and to God, we volunteered anyway.

Our offer was accepted and, shortly thereafter, we began learning the details of several situations we had not known before. When we started addressing these problems and concerns, we became the targets of rocks, spears and blowguns from all sides.

It had seemed like the right thing to do, but we should have stayed in the middle of the posse and low in the saddle. Ultimately, we retreated to lick our wounds and to never volunteer in that church again.

Until you know you have the support and protection of the others in your group, stay in the middle of the posse and low in the saddle.

LESSONS:

1. You cannot resuscitate a dead horse.

2. Don't try to win races with plow horses, and don't try to plow fields with thoroughbreds.

3. When you are in a new set of circumstances, a new organization or with a new herd, take time to learn before you speak and act.

TIPS:

1. When the horse, relationship, situation or mistake is dead, let it go and move on.

2. Don't play to just get tired!

3. Work hard to assess whether you have a real thoroughbred on your team or just a really likable plow horse.

4. Until you know you have the support and protection of the others in the herd, stay in the middle of the posse and low in the saddle.

CHAPTER II

EQUIPPING YOURSELF FOR JUNGLE TRAVEL

"The biggest secret to success is this:
There is no secret to success."

HUBBARD

Like any other travel, preparing for your journey into the jungle should include equipping yourself for the trip.

Aside from understanding the ways of the jungle itself, you'll need sturdy footwear and appropriate clothing for these temperate treks. You'll also need knowledge of the various species you'll encounter as well as the right tools, road maps and, of course, survival skills.

During and after my professional career, I have maintained several large folders. They contain my own notes and writings of all types and from many sources – inspirational pathways and footbridges. I review the folders' contents a couple of times each year to refresh my memory and recharge my batteries.

In this chapter, I'll share some of my favorite pathways and footbridges that have made it possible for me to safely travel through unknown jungles over the past 40 years. At least, I think you'll find these pathways and footbridges make it easier to move ahead.

During my many folder reviews, I've found that – although different in format, context and length – the contents share timelessness and consistency.

I have included some of the older items throughout the book to demonstrate that the basic messages never change. What frequently changes, as the world perceives itself to be smarter and more sophisticated, is how long it takes to state the message.

The pathways and footbridges I have included in this chapter have the advantage of brevity, making them easy to read and to remember. They are but a few in my collection.

Here are a few of my pathways and bridges:

Embrace technology and use it to your advantage. Using technology is like breathing in today's business arena – you have to do it to survive.

———————————

Learn correct English and use it to your advantage. The use of correct English allows you to make good first impressions and separate yourself from others who do not have your language skills. It also gives you the ability to make your points effectively and express your expectations clearly so you can get more from your team.

———————————

Learn to communicate in as many languages as possible and as soon as possible. Knowing several languages gives you the ability to communicate with others in our shrinking global world.

No matter your age, be respectful of others. Say the following phrases often: "Yes, Sir/Ma'am," "No, Sir/Ma'am," "Please," "Thank you," "Good morning," "Good evening," "Excuse me" and "I apologize." Like using correct English, the ability to say these phrases in other languages will also set you apart and make your life easier in the global jungle.

Learn about other cultures and respect them.

The biggest secret to learning or remembering something is the desire to do so.

Don't hesitate to try new and different things – foods, activities, sports, travels. You'll be more respected and accepted, and you will enjoy life more if you are open to new experiences.

Control your vices NOW!

Learn to dance well! But be careful who you dance with and who you allow to dance with you.

———————————

Look for potentially great people and mentor them to greatness. You'll learn more than you teach.

———————————

You cannot get where you want to go if you never start.

———————————

If it's stupid but works, it's not stupid.

———————————

The easy path is usually mined with explosive situations. Watch for the unexpected.

———————————

Don't be afraid to take action. Anything you do can get you shot – especially doing nothing.

———————————

In Chapter 7, I referred to Bill Gates' rules about living in the real world. They were contained in a speech given to high school students on the subject, "Things They Did Not and Will Not Teach You in School," originally penned by Charles J. Sykes. Here is the complete list:

Rule 1: Life is not fair – get used to it!

Rule 2: The world won't care about your self-esteem. The world will expect you to accomplish something **before** you feel good about yourself.

Rule 3: You will NOT make $60,000 a year right out of high school. You won't be a vice president with a car phone until you earn both.

Rule 4: If you think your teacher is tough, wait until you get a boss.

Rule 5: Flipping burgers is not beneath your dignity. Your grandparents had a different word for burger-flipping – they called it opportunity.

Rule 6: If you mess up, it's not your parents' fault, so don't whine about your mistakes – learn from them.

Rule 7: Before you were born, your parents weren't as boring as they are now. They got that way from paying your bills, cleaning your clothes and listening to you talk about how cool you thought you were. So before you save the rain forest from the parasites of your parents' generation, try delousing the closet in your own room.

Rule 8: Your school may have done away with winners and losers but life has not. In some schools, they have abolished failing grades and they'll give you as many times as you want to get the right answer. This doesn't bear the slightest resemblance to **anything** in real life.

Rule 9: Life is not divided into semesters. You don't get summers off and very few employers are interested in helping you find yourself. Do that on your own time.

Rule 10: Television is NOT real life. In real life, people actually have to leave the coffee shop and go to jobs.

Rule 11: Be nice to nerds. Chances are you'll end up working for one.

I have six favorite secular books that I re-read and refer to often. I have mentioned two of them already. For your convenience, here is the list in chronological order and not necessarily the order of impact on my life or journey:

+ *Rhinoceros Success* – Scott Alexander, 1980

+ *The One Minute Manager* – Kenneth Blanchard and Spencer Johnson, 1981

+ *All I Really Need to Know I Learned in Kindergarten* – Robert Fulghum, 1989

+ *Tuesdays With Morrie* – Mitch Albom, 1997

+ *Who Moved My Cheese?* – Spencer Johnson, 1998

+ *Orchestrating Attitude* – Lee Colan, 2005

There is a seventh book that stands far above the rest in order of importance to me. I get my best guidance and direction from the Bible. Therefore, it is in the Bible that I find my best pathways and bridges.

Unlike the other chapters, this chapter does not end with lessons and tips. You can decide for yourself how best to equip yourself for the journey, what vaccinations you may need, what words of wisdom to use when you're in survival mode, what pathways and bridges to use and what lessons to learn on your own personal safaris.

Ultimately, I hope that my lessons will serve as valuable tools as you continue your day-to-day encounters with the animals who inhabit your own personal jungles. And as you travel, spend some time along the way sharing these and other lessons with fellow travelers.

Today's jungles are ruthless, competitive and unforgiving. May my lessons make your journey less difficult as you travel toward your professional and personal success.

NEW SAFARIS

Gullible's travels through life's jungle continue at a hurried pace and he continues to learn new lessons and to revalidate others. One of those lessons is "Life is what you make it."

I'm still surrounded by all types of people. Some are happy and some are sad. Some are active and some are bored. Some are sick and some are well. All are different.

I see the people around me making all kinds of choices. Some are wise ... some not so wise. With the exception of those who are very ill, every person is what he or she chooses to be.

Happiness is a choice ... just like unhappiness, laziness, boredom, selfishness and serving others! I have chosen to be happy and active and to have a great time on my life's safaris.

The lessons and tips contained in this book can be applied to all of life's jungles. The seamless life does not end at the end of any safari until the last one. It continues even if the jungle or the safari changes.

I encourage every reader, regardless of age, to stay active, lead the seamless life, balance the four P's, do what's right, and to use your leadership talents and skills and help others until your last safari ends.

Be a person of integrity who helps a few others along the way.

May God bless you and keep you safe on your journey.

Gullible's Travels is dedicated to
my talented, kind and faithful friend,
Bill Jones
1942-2008

ABOUT THE AUTHOR

Topper Long's business life began at the age of 11 when he started mowing neighbors' lawns for a few dollars. His formal business career ended 46 years later when he retired as CEO of Textron Engine Marine and Land Systems, a $400 million collection of three companies, two of which he was also President. During those years, he earned a BS degree in Engineering and a MS degree in Executive Management. He served as an officer in the U.S. Army and worked 17 years in government service and 17 years in private industry.

Topper and his wife, Carole, divide their time between homes in Gallatin, Tennessee, and Valle Crucis, North Carolina. They have two daughters, two sons-in-law and four grandchildren, all who have been some of Topper's best mentors.

It was during his 47 years of traveling though the jungles of government, corporate America and many other segments of life that Topper, a wide-eyed gullible traveler, learned the lessons in this book.

Gullible may be contacted at gulliblestravels@comcast.net and is available for presentations, seminars or consulting regarding his travels in the business jungle.

I extend my sincere appreciation and admiration
to all those who inspired and encouraged me
to write this book, with special thanks to
Lee Colan for his valuable advice, and to
Alice Adams for her encouragement and untiring efforts.

A CHAPTER-BY-CHAPTER COMPLETE QUICK REFERENCE GUIDE TO LEADERSHIP LESSONS AND TIPS

CHAPTER 1: Flying Over the Jungle

LESSONS:

1. Perceptions are realities to their owners.

2. People relate to you based on their perceptions – and not on your intentions.

3. It is extremely important to know the perceptions of those you're leading.

4. Make sure the perceptions, intentions and realities are things you are proud for others to notice.

TIPS:

1. Fly over the jungle – and pay attention to what you see below.

2. Surround yourself with your "BEST" team and listen to them.

3. Honestly learn how people perceive you – to see yourself as others see you.

4. Have the honesty, humility, courage and determination to change your behavior and to match the perceptions of others with your intentions and to reality.

CHAPTER 2: Seamless Living

LESSONS:

1. Be true to yourself.

2. You never know whom you are influencing ... or when or where.

3. The key to happiness and contentment is living a seamless life.

4. The seamless life is one life – business, family, church, social – all the same life.

TIPS:

1. Think and decide today what you want on your tombstone.

2. Write down what you want on your tombstone and post reminders everywhere.

3. Become guided by what you have written – all day, every day.

4. Fly over your jungle, using your BEST team to keep your seamless life seamless, and live so that what you want on your tombstone will eventually be inscribed on it.

CHAPTER 3: Balancing the Four P's

LESSONS:

1. Making Progress, seeking Perfection, Pulling Together, and having a Positive Attitude are key ingredients for having a happy, seamless life and productive career.

2. Achieving and maintaining BALANCE among the Four P's is the secret to the success of the process.

TIPS:

1. Find, cultivate and use good guides as you travel through the jungle.

2. Spend time analyzing the weight each of the Four P's has in all of your "lives."

3. Balance! Balance! Balance!

CHAPTER 4: Progress: Riding a Rhino

LESSONS:

1. "I didn't have time" and "I forgot" are not good reasons or excuses.

2. The biggest impediment to progress is resistance to change.

3. Nothing of significance happens as a result of anything less than a crisis.

4. The environment is going to get you. Unexpected things will happen to change plans and impede progress.

5. There is an appropriate size and formality of management structure for every organization.

6. Keep charging!

TIPS:

1. Change "I didn't have time" to "I did not choose to use my time for that because ...."

2. Use a pencil and paper to eliminate the "I forgot" excuse.

3. Don't waste your valuable time with people who don't want to make progress.

4. Overcome inertia. Determine to make progress before a crisis.

5. Expect the unexpected.

6. Define and state tasks well for yourself and your team.

CHAPTER 5: Perfection: Good Enough Is Not Good Enough

LESSONS:

1. Anything worth spending your most precious and limited resource on is worth doing right.

2. You usually get at least one level of quality below what you expect.

3. Your brain is like a muscle. If you don't use it, you lose it.

4. Life is a test program in which there will be both failure and success.

5. You will never have all of the information on anything. Start anyway.

TIPS:

1. Strive for perfection because you want to.

2. Think ahead. Skate to where the puck is going to be.

3. Exercise your brain and keep it sharp.

4. Acknowledge mistakes, learn from failures, recover, and move on quickly.

5. Don't succumb to "analysis paralysis."

CHAPTER 6: Pulling Together: There Are No Justa's

LESSONS:

1. Some people refuse to pull together, and those people are dangerous.

2. There are no "little people" or "justa's" on a good team.

3. A leader can give away authority but not responsibility.

4. Even in unpleasant times, people react according to how they are treated.

5. 100/100 works better than 50/50.

TIPS:

1. Don't allow those who will not pull together to change your course or stop your progress.

2. Treat no one as a "justa."

3. Stay within the boundaries of your position.

4. Get to know, care about and respect other team members.

5. Give your 100 percent willingly.

6. Pay attention to the Ten Commandments of How to Get Along With People.

7. Criticize behaviors, not people.

CHAPTER 7: Positive Attitude: Whether Quarters or Millions

LESSONS:

1. When faced with adversity, we can become a carrot, an egg or a coffee bean.

2. Our attitude determines our altitude and affects the attitude of those around us.

3. Life is not fair. Don't expect it to be.

4. The Attitude Self-Evaluation is a valuable tool for developing a positive attitude.

5. When we are dissatisfied or angry, we have only two choices: Get happy or die mad.

TIPS:

1. Work at being coffee instead of a carrot or an egg.

2. Make your actions determine your circumstances, and take advantage of those circumstances today.

3. Accept that life is not fair. Keep a positive attitude anyway.

4. If you can't enjoy what you are doing most of the time, do something else.

5. Sometimes you have to "fake it until you make it" to regain a positive attitude.

6. Work at answering "Yes" to all of the Attitude Self-Evaluation questions.

7. Choose to get happy rather than to die mad.

CHAPTER 8: The Changing Laws of the Jungle

LESSONS:

1. I must be ready to die at any moment … because I might.

2. The fact that you think what you are doing is right does not make it right.

3. Prejudice and discrimination – based on things another cannot change – are wrong.

4. You can no longer assume everybody defines "doing what's right" the same way you do.

TIPS:

1. Continually assess your actions against your values. If they don't match, change your actions.

2. Assess people based on how they behave, contribute and perform.

3. Fix problems quickly, based on facts, and move on.

4. Decide what your principles are and stick to them.

5. Learn what others believe before assuming they agree with you.

Chapter 9: At the Head of the Pack

Lessons:

1. Good leaders never stop learning and improving.

2. Your success as a leader depends on others' perception of you, the nature of the task and your ability to do it.

3. When you take responsibility quickly, you build valuable capital and gain respect.

4. When you take blame that doesn't permanently hurt you, you save time and energy ... and it may get you valuable points.

5. People live both up and down to your expectations.

Tips:

1. Never stop your on-the-job training and your quest for self-improvement.

2. Give the credit and take the blame ... if it is not going to get you killed. It saves time and energy.

3. Criticize the behavior, not the person, unless the person deserves the criticism.

4. Be nice on your way up. You may come down the same ladder.

5. Give respect and good service to those who pay you, and demand respect and good service from those you are paying.

CHAPTER 10: Horses in the Jungle?

LESSONS:

1. You cannot resuscitate a dead horse.

2. Don't try to win races with plow horses, and don't try to plow fields with thoroughbreds.

3. When you are in a new set of circumstances, a new organization or with a new herd, take time to learn before you speak and act.

TIPS:

1. When the horse, relationship, situation or mistake is dead, let it go and move on.

2. Don't play to just get tired!

3. Work hard to assess whether you have a real thoroughbred on your team or just a really likable plow horse.

4. Until you know you have the support and protection of the others in the herd, stay in the middle of the posse and low in the saddle.

Introducing 7 Spectacular New CornerStone Posters, Note Cards & Desktop Prints

These dramatic, inspiring posters and note cards will continually remind and reflect the importance of your organization's values!

To view the entire collection that includes 19 amazing images, visit www.CornerStoneLeadership.com

Accelerate Personal Growth Package
$139.95

Visit www.**CornerStoneLeadership**.com for additional books and resources.

☑ YES! Please send me extra copies of *Gullible's Travels!*
1-30 copies $14.95   31-100 copies $13.95   101+ copies $12.95

Gullible's Travels	_____ copies X _____	= $ _____

Additional Personal Growth Resources

Accelerate Personal Growth Package   _____ pack(s) X $139.95   = $ _____
   (Includes one each of all items pictured
   on page 118.)

Other Books

_____   _____ copies X _____   = $ _____

_____   _____ copies X _____   = $ _____

_____   _____ copies X _____   = $ _____

_____   _____ copies X _____   = $ _____

_____   _____ copies X _____   = $ _____

        Shipping & Handling $ _____

               Subtotal $ _____

     Sales Tax (8.25%-TX Only) $ _____

     Total (U.S. Dollars Only)   **$ _____**

Shipping and Handling Charges

Total $ Amount	Up to $49	$50-$99	$100-$249	$250-$1199	$1200-$2999	$3000+
Charge	$7	$9	$16	$30	$80	$125

Name _____ Job Title_____

Organization _____ Phone_____

Shipping Address _____ Fax_____

Billing Address_____ E-mail _____
                                      (required when ordering PowerPoint® Presentation)

City_____ State _____ ZIP_____

❑ Please invoice (Orders over $200) Purchase Order Number (if applicable)_____

Charge Your Order: ❑ MasterCard   ❑ Visa   ❑ American Express

Credit Card Number _____ Exp. Date_____

Signature _____

❑ Check Enclosed (Payable to: CornerStone Leadership)

Fax	**Mail**	**Phone**
972.274.2884	P.O. Box 764087	888.789.5323
	Dallas, TX 75376	

www.**CornerStoneLeadership**.com

Thank you for reading *Gullible's Travels*.
We hope it has assisted you in your quest for
personal and professional growth.

CornerStone Leadership is committed to providing new
and enlightening products to organizations worldwide.
Our mission is to fuel knowledge with practical resources
that will accelerate your team's productivity,
success and job satisfaction!

Best wishes for your continued success.

CornerStone
Leadership Institute
www.CornerStoneLeadership.com

*Start a crusade in your organization —
have the courage to learn, the vision to lead,
and the passion to share.*